*A collection of life stories based in
faith, justice, and truth*

WISDOM
tales

JAMES BLIESE WHITE

ISBN: 9798842773749

Published by Writer's Tablet, LLC

WritersTablet.org

DEDICATION

I dedicate this book to my lovely and loving wife Catherine Mathis White, who has cared for me for more than 50 years.

CONTENTS

ACKNOWLEDGMENT

The people who served as beta readers to make sure I was speaking clearly to my "barbershop crowd" deserve a lot of credit. A thousand thanks to those who made suggestions and read the manuscripts: Catherine White, Tasha Robertson, Spencer Robertson, Morgan Robertson, Cora Wilder, Mary Gholston. Thanks to my proof-readers: Girtha Perkins and Sandra Jones.

I also appreciate all of the professional support of the publishers, Writer's Tablet Agency.

INTRODUCTION

Wisdom Tales is based on teachings from the ancient African Wisdom Tradition (AWT), a tradition that began with the establishment of a priesthood that included both men and women. No one knows exactly when it began, but research suggests that 37,000 years ago is a reasonable guess. This means that "Black History" did not start in 1619 in North America. It began even before the great pyramids were built. In fact, it provided the knowledge that made the pyramids possible.

The main goal of the African Wisdom Tradition is to change how we think. It is not trying to provide information. If I wanted to provide information, I would have written a 300-page book with footnotes. As a "Wisdom-Priest-in-Training," my goal is to change your consciousness. I try to correct wrong ideas and misinformation. Our schools have misled us. I want you, dear reader, to rid yourself of the wrong understanding you got in school.

The African Wisdom Tradition teaches that all things are sacred. We can learn from the smallest things – indeed, sometimes the smallest things reveal to us the deepest truths. We can also learn from what other people did at other times and in other places.

I address this book to you, my "barbershop crowd" at the House of Styles.

Who am I?

Having pursued graduate studies in sociology and theology, I not only taught sociology in college to earn a living, but I also served as an unpaid pastor of a beautiful congregation in Harlem. In addition, I worked part-time as a national program consultant for many church denominations. I was very active in the civil rights movement of the 1960's. I even went to the Republic of South Africa to research and report on the evils of apartheid.

A native of Harlem, I was a disorganized but successful student in the public school system. My family were professional musicians on my mother's side, while my father was a precision machinist.

I am married with three children and two grandchildren. I like to play chess.

BIBLE
Wisdom

LADY WISDOM

While creating the universe, Creator followed a set of design rules. One rule said that everything had to be balanced and in harmony like beautiful music. Another rule said that good behavior was required in all relationships among all people. There were many other rules that made the universe grow into a work of art. Creator called the set of rules "Lady Wisdom." Lady Wisdom was like a library with a record of all the rules that Creator wanted followed.

After the stars were formed into great galaxies, Creator formed humanity on planet Earth. Inside a large place called Eden, Creator planted a garden. Creator assigned humanity as caretakers of planet Earth. Creator did not want human beings to be robots. Humanity had to be free to make independent decisions. That way, love for Creator would be freely and sincerely given. Love of Creator had to be a choice. Otherwise, it would not be genuine love.

There were 1,000 trees in the garden that was located in Eden. Humanity had the right to eat from 999 trees. But Creator said that there was one tree that must not be touched. One tree was in honor of Creator. The odds were 999 to 1 that humanity would pass the test. But mankind failed. How do we explain the mistake?

Here's how: humanity wanted to be equal to Creator. Humanity wanted to make all the rules.

But Creator loved humanity too much to give up on human beings. Creator sent Lady Wisdom, the set of rules, to help. If humanity learned and followed the rules of Lady Wisdom, humanity would live a joyous life with four things: love for Creator; love for our inner selves; love for one another, and love for nature.

Lady Wisdom got busy. She visited the descendants of Ham and taught them astronomy and how to build giant pyramids. She went to Europe, began a rebirth of understanding, and guided the construction of the cathedrals. She taught the Native Indians of North America about the sacred beauty of nature. Lady Wisdom went all over the world visiting factories, farms, art studios, laboratories, and classrooms.

She appeared under different names. Sometimes she was called Compassion. Sometimes Patience, sometimes Grace, sometimes Understanding, sometimes Know-how, sometimes Gratitude, sometimes Generosity, sometimes Global Education, sometimes Neighborly Kindness, sometimes Democracy.

Some people accepted Lady Wisdom. Those who agreed with Lady Wisdom believed that by working together, humanity could achieve more happiness than if each person worked alone.

Other people refused to befriend Lady Wisdom. They thought their ideas were better. They thought that they could bring more happiness to themselves by taking away the happiness of others.

As you listen to the following tales, each of you must decide whether you agree or disagree with me. You see, I am Lady Wisdom.

<u>NEXT</u>

I would like to introduce you to my Boss, but that will have to wait till the next session.

WHICH NAME?

Does God have a name?

Not really.

But I've heard many names for God.

A personal name is needed only when there are many things of the same kind. Since there is only one Creator, we don't have to call the Creator by a personal name like Susan or George.

What about Jehovah?

Wrong spelling.

How about "Jehovah Jireh"?

That's a title, not a personal name.

How about "Emmanuel"?

That describes the divine presence. It is not a personal name.

Could we not use "The Almighty"?

Another title. The Bible has many titles. But the function, the power, the purpose is creation.

Why do people insist on calling God by a personal name?

Because when we know someone's personal name, we can use it. It makes us feel like we have a close relationship to that person.

According to the Bible, there must be some name, right?

The Hebrew word YHWH is based on a verb. A verb is an action word and a word indicating existence. It is strong and stable. It is not a noun. Nouns are either titles or personal names.

What does the verb YHWH mean?

It means the "Creator Who Is Present." The Creator makes things come into existence that did not exist before. And Creator is present with us.

Is that the way the Bible talks about the deity?

Yes. Always. The Bible begins by saying "In the beginning the deity created the heavens and the earth." That statement means that everything that exists came into being by the power of the Creator.

The universe is mighty big. That's a lot of creating.

Creators create. That's what they do. They are not copycats always repeating the same things. Remember Duke Ellington, Mozart, and Toni Morrison. They kept creating new works of art.

How did it begin?

Everything started when the Creator said, "Let there be light." That speck of light expanded into the universe.

You are talking about a very big deity.

Yes. People often think of the deity as too small. They try to fit all of their ideas about the Creator into their human brain.

Is that why you avoid using the word "God" in your writing?

Yes. Too many people have destroyed the word. Too often it has been used for selfish purposes. Using the word "Creator" makes it more difficult to shrink the deity to human size. It also keeps us focused on the central activity of ongoing creation. Every snowflake, every leaf is a new creation. Creating is intelligent, ongoing, and purposeful.

If the Creator is bigger than the universe, where do things go when they no longer exist? What happens when something is totally destroyed?

Nothing is ever totally destroyed. Let's take an example. A log burning in the fireplace turns into ashes. The heat energy continues to float out of the room, out of the house, into the universe. Scientists tell us nothing is ever completely destroyed, only transformed. The ashes remain behind, but the energy continues to travel out.

What about the ashes?

They will be transformed slowly into chemical components.

Is the Creator aware of all these transformations?

Yes.

What about you and me?

What do you mean?

What happens when we die? Are we transformed also? Is the Creator aware of us? Does the Creator even care about the tiny creatures that we are?

The Bible teaches us that Creator has prepared a special place for us. The Bible does not describe what that place is like. It only assures us that the place is more glorious than we are able to imagine.

NEXT

Now that we have been introduced to the Boss, what is required of us? We shall learn in the next session.

WISDOM SYMBOL

"Hey, She, why are you watching the lions drinking from the Nile River?"

"We must not only see," said She, "we must also observe. The lions reveal that our intelligent Creator has made them intelligent too. They live in families and know how to care for one another. We could learn from them."

"You are a worthy priest, She."

Sheshat was a young woman from a moderate-income African family. Her friend was Imhotep. His was a poor African family. The two of them had just entered the Ancient African Priesthood of Wisdom. Sheshat called her childhood friend Mo. He called her She.

"Our priesthood has also taught us to make sure that everything on Earth agrees with everything in the heavens. Creator's will must be done on Earth as it is done in Heaven."

"Yes, Mo, but how can we teach others that truth?"

"Maybe build a monument, She."

"Great idea, Mo. But it must be big, and it must last for thousands of years. The truth is so important. A symbol of wise living, reminding everyone to love our Maker, love ourselves, and love our neighbor."

"So, it would have to be three-sided."

"Yes, just like the triangles that helped our priests to measure how far away the stars are. The triangles that enable them to find their way across the oceans."

"We use little triangles to mark the graves of our loved ones."

"The monument will have to be forty stories tall."

"Yes, very big."

Then the young woman She and the young man Mo worked through the night digging a trench. Their muscles ached but they kept working. Mo and She filled the trench with water. They knew that water always finds its own level.

"Now our building will be level like the water."

"Yes. We have to make our building agree with the heavens to honor Creator. Let's use a rope, Mo. You take one end and face me. You will be facing north. I will take the other end facing south," said She.

"Pull tight!"

"Swing the rope a little to the right. Make the rope parallel with the eastern star."

"Look up at the Milky Way stars. "

"Point the rope to the equinox."

"Now our building will be level and face the right direction."

"Call the builders!"

The project required three decades of work. Thirty years from when She and Mo began, the forty-story building was done. The citizens, not any slaves, had done the job. Its polished white stone cover gleamed in the sunlight. It could be seen from twenty miles away.

People greatly respected them. They called her "Old Woman She" and her friend "Old Man Mo." The two elderly friends kneeled together at the foot of their structure. They gave thanks to their Almighty Creator. Their great wisdom symbol would last.

Today, 4,000 years later, it is considered one of the Seven Wonders of the Ancient World. The building stands by the Nile River, where the lion family drank. The three sides of the building will remind everyone that love is three-sided. We must love our Creator, love ourselves, and love our neighbor.

Today, we call the building of Sheshat and Imhotep "The Great Pyramid of Giza."

NEXT

Love is for everyone. That is why Jesus rejected custom and selected women to be his disciples. He did not limit himself to men. In the next session, we shall discover one of Jesus' women disciples.

WHAT WAS HER NAME?

Who was the woman who became a disciple of Jesus and assisted his ministry from beginning to end? Well, her career started like this:

Her son was dying. The boy was stretched out in front of her and her husband, Chudza. Chudza was the chief of staff and finance minister of the king. The couple had hired many renowned doctors to tend to their son, yet the little fellow was on his death bed.

"Saddle Stallion!" Chudza ordered. "Honey, I'm going to see Jesus. He's back from Jerusalem and when he was there, they say he healed sick people."

"Do you think he is the Messiah?" she asked.

"I pray so."

Chudza galloped Stallion hard, trying to cover the 20 miles from Capernaum to Cana fast. But no horse can gallop at full speed for that distance. Chudza had to stop every five miles to rest Stallion by allowing him to walk or trot.

Up, up through the hill country to Cana, where Jesus had turned water into wine. "Will Jesus come to my house and heal my son?"

The question rose from his heart as his voice threw it into the wind.

Stallion was breathing hard. Chudza feared for his health as they arrived at the house. A crowd had gathered to see Jesus. "Let me through! I must speak to Jesus!" Chudza struggled through the crowd.

Chudza fell before Jesus and said, "Jesus, please come to my house. My son is dying."

Jesus tested Chudza by saying, "Some people will not believe the Creator unless they see a miracle."

Chudza persisted, "Lord Jesus, my little boy is about to die!" Chudza did not ask to see anything. Jesus was impressed by Chudza's faith and said, "Your son shall live."

Chudza looked into the face of the Lord and believed.

Stallion was exhausted, so Chudza could not ride him back immediately. He allowed Stallion to rest overnight. They left in the morning. He was halfway home when his servants met him with the exciting news that his son had revived. The assistants knew Chudza. They knew what he would ask because he was a man always conscious of time. "What time did the fever leave him?"

His servants said, "One o'clock yesterday afternoon." It was in fact one o'clock when Jesus had said, "Your son shall live." Chudza then knew for sure that Jesus was the Messiah.

At home, his household celebrated the healing by Jesus from 20 miles away. At last, after 400 years of waiting, the Messiah had come.

The child's mother agreed with her husband that she would go to Jesus. She would do something disallowed by their laws, their traditions, and customs. A woman, this grateful mother, would ask to enroll in The School of Jesus.

Jesus welcomed her as one of his private students, one of his special disciples.

Her name was Joanna.

<u>NEXT</u>

In the following session, we shall discover a relative who was a woman disciple of Jesus.

FRIENDSHIP

I went to get her. A child of 15. Elizabeth had cared for her through her pregnancy. But now what? Her husband, my husband's brother, is old. Mary will outlive Joseph. My husband Clopas and I decided to help Mother Mary.

Creator has made Clopas very successful in business. With such success comes much responsibility. "Tell her to lean on you," said Clopas.

Mother Mary had to bear up under much criticism. Rumors flew against her. Although virgin births happen in the animal kingdom and insect kingdom all the time, many people do not believe that Creator can do the same for humans. Cruel tongues lashed at her from every side. I said, "Let them come at me!"

Jesus grew up and became a carpenter. Every son learned his father's trade.

Joseph died. Jesus began his public ministry.

I travelled with Mother Mary. We went to the small town of Cana. We helped prepare a wedding celebration that would last for days. Jesus was invited. People drank so heavily that the wine supply ran out. Mary went to Jesus for help. He provided more wine from the water tub. The word spread and many people began to believe that he was the Messiah.

Throughout the three years of Jesus' ministry, Mary suffered from fear. She was afraid that his enemies would destroy him. How could he survive the Judean power structure? They had their spies everywhere. The Judeans were supported by the Romans. They had most of the wealth. They controlled the Temple in Jerusalem.

Why did the Judeans want to destroy Jesus? The Judeans were afraid that Jesus would take away their power. All the people were willing to follow Jesus.

Throughout the three years, I reminded Mother Mary to lean on me. I stood by her when Jesus raised Lazarus from the dead. I was with her when we celebrated the last Passover in the upper room. I prayed with her in the Garden of Gethsemane. We trembled and wept together at the foot of the cross. Mother Mary held on to my arm as we walked behind the body to the tomb. We hugged when we discovered the empty tomb. I spoke for her when we reported to the men. I held her when we received final instructions from our risen Lord. How happy I am that Mother Mary leaned on me.

After his resurrection, Jesus thanked me and Clopas for supporting his Mother Mary. The risen Messiah honored us by escorting me and Clopas all the way home to Emmaus.

NEXT

Some of Jesus' women disciples did not travel with him. Nevertheless, they were enrolled in "The School of Jesus." Who were they? The answer will become clear in the next session.

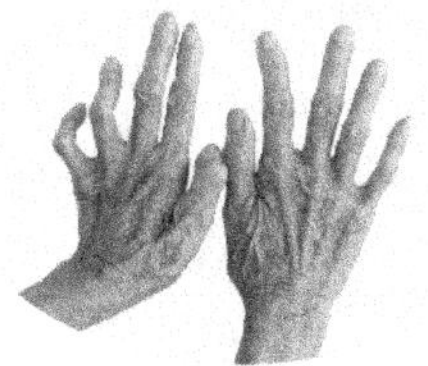

MARTHA'S HOUSE

Her face was ugly. Leprosy had turned her into a monster. Whenever she walked down the road the law required her to yell, "Leper! Leper!" Children ran away and hid. Adults turned their heads. She was forbidden to visit the Temple in Jerusalem. The ugly woman decided to go and talk to Martha. She heard that Jesus had raised a man named Lazarus from the dead. Lazarus had died from leprosy. He was a brother of Martha. The ugly woman thought that if Jesus could raise a leper from the dead, he could cure her face.

Martha's house was always very busy. People were coming and going all the time. That is why when the woman with the ugly face knocked on Martha's door, Martha invited her in. Martha told the leper lady to lie on a cot and rest. Martha knew what she needed. Martha had suffered the same problem. "Jesus is not here at the moment. He is visiting Simon the leper. He will be back soon."

Mary, the sister of Martha, came into the room. Mary said that she was worried because the authorities were looking to arrest Jesus. Mary wondered why the people in power wanted to destroy the Messiah.

Martha explained the reason. Martha said that after Jesus raised Lazarus from the dead, he then rode on a donkey into Jerusalem. Crowds gathered around him and welcomed him as a king. After

Jesus got into the city, he went to the Temple. The bankers with their tables were open for business. It was the custom that when the bankers closed in the evening, they would overturn their own tables. They placed them on their sides to indicate to people that they were closed. Jesus went into the Temple, overturned the tables, and said, "You are now out of business." The bankers and the authorities made a lot of money from cheating the people. Jesus was interrupting their cashflow. In a loud voice, Jesus said, "This Temple is supposed to be a house of prayer. But you have turned it into a den of robbers."

Martha said, "The Temple leaders were already angry at Jesus, so they developed a plan to arrest him. They wanted him crucified by the Romans." Martha's explanation helped Mary and the ugly woman to understand.

Just then, Jesus returned from Simon's house. He sat on a stool. Mary took the position of a disciple. She happily sat at his feet to learn. Martha got busy cooking. She complained that her sister Mary was supposed to help her. But Jesus said that for a woman to seek an education was more urgent than to fix a meal.

As Ugly Leper Lady listened to the teachings of Jesus, she began to feel different. She touched her face with her hand. The scars were gone. Her skin was smooth. Her face was no longer twisted. She was healed.

Martha cooked a lot of food. The small house was filled with the sweet aroma of compassion. She was accustomed to having a lot of people visit. Martha understood that people came to her house seeking the Messiah.

Although Martha had been healed and was no longer sick, she did not plan to leave Bethany. She understood that it was her calling to provide a place for the sick and dying.

NEXT

Another woman disciple had a truly historic impact on the Christian movement. She was "the apostle to the apostles." Who was she? This superstar is next.

MAGDALA

You smelled it before you saw it. The town was known for its fish industry. But it was also known as home of a woman who was crazy. Her insanity destroyed the quality of her life.

Jesus continued walking along the shore of the Sea of Galilee. He was on a mission. The mission was to save an important woman. He was going to her to give her the calling on her life.

Her name was Mary. She was so mentally sick that they described her as seven-times sick. But her disease was no match for the healing powers of Jesus. Jesus brought her from the depths of despair. She thanked him by accepting her calling. She became a disciple traveling to save others like herself. No demon was going to stop her. She would fulfill her responsibility.

Jesus distinguished Mary from all the other "Marys" in the region. He called her by her town name, Magdala. As a young adult, she deserved her own affectionate name. Jesus saw leadership inside her. And she did not disappoint him. Whenever he needed someone to rally the other women disciples, he could count on her. She mobilized the group.

As they went from village to town to city to countryside, Magdala went into the homes to spread the gospel. The culture socially segregated men from women. That is why men disciples were not allowed to enter homes. The women had to do it.

When they approached a town, Magdala gathered the families together a day ahead of time. She told everyone to come and hear Jesus.

Her courage made her the spokesperson for Joanna, Susanna, Mary of Clopas, Salome, and all the other women who were private disciples of Jesus. They recognized her ability in spite of her youth.

She was at the forefront of every major event in the ministry of Jesus.

She was even at the cross when the soldiers were doing their work of crucifixion. She walked in the processional behind Mother Mary and the pallbearers. She watched as they rolled the hand-carved circular stone into the slot in the ground. She knew that the men disciples would not know where to find the tomb. She memorized its location.

She shopped for the spices to place on the body of Jesus.

She outran the middle-aged women to the tomb in the darkness of Sunday morning.

She was the first to see the empty tomb. At the empty tomb, the resurrected Jesus called her "Mary." She had not heard her real name in years. When Magdala heard her true name, she yelled, "My teacher!" She was not his girlfriend; she was his student.

She took the message of the empty tomb to Peter. She led Peter and John to the empty tomb.

Then she led the women back to Galilee to meet with their risen Lord.

It was Mary from Magdala who witnessed the entire ministry of Jesus. She became the Creator's primary eyewitness to the key events in the history of the Incarnation.

For the rest of her life, the woman people today call Mary Magdalene was in demand as a speaker. Historians called her "apostle to the apostles."

Before she was healed, Magdala had been considered last in Galilee. Jesus healed her and made her first in the empire. No disciple was more important to the early Christian movement than Magdala. Her beautiful life spread a sweet aroma across the world.

NEXT

Christians could not meet in the synagogues on Saturdays. The authorities wanted to arrest them. So, the Christian movement met in homes. But which day did they celebrate the Sabbath? Is the issue "a big fight over a small thing"?

THE LORD'S DAY

You said that I am liable to go to hell if I don't worship on Saturday. I ask you, which day of the week did Moses celebrate the Sabbath?

I have not been able to find the answer to that question. Does anybody know?

Saturday was a Roman holiday. Also, the Romans had an eight-day week.

Since their week was eight days long, it is not the same as our week.

It's a hard question.

We know that Moses did not have a Roman calendar because the Romans did not exist in his day.

Is there anything wrong with following the Roman calendar?

Today, it's OK to use it for practical purposes. But on Sunday, the Romans worshiped the sun. On Monday, the moon. Tuesday was for the god Tiu. Wednesday was for Wodin. Thursday was dedicated to Thor. Friday was in honor of the goddess Frei. Saturday was for Saturn. No Roman day was set aside for Jesus.

How did the early Christians handle it?

They worshiped after work. They called the Sabbath "Kuriake" which means "the Lord's Day."

You still have not answered the question.

Yes, I have. Christians celebrated whenever they got off from work.

Which day?

Whenever they got off from work.

The Bible says Jesus and Paul went into the synagogue on the Sabbath. Wasn't that Saturday?

Perhaps. But not our Saturday. It was a different calendar.

You are confusing me.

You are confused because you think that the Sabbath is tied to a specific calendar. There have been as many calendars as cultures. Which one is right?

There have been a lot of calendars throughout history?

Yes. And remember, when it is one day in one part of the world, it is a different day in a different part of the world. When it is Friday in the United States, it is Saturday in Japan.

True.

Even within the same country, it is difficult to worship together.

What do you mean?

In the United States, when we were farmers, everyone milked their cows and plowed their fields at the same time of day. Having everybody attend church services at the same time on the same day was easy.

You're right. My grandpa had a farm in Mississippi. I visited one summer. Everybody did the same thing at the same time on the same day.

Yes. But in the city, we all have different schedules and responsibilities. Forcing people into one day and one hour causes difficulties.

I guess you're right.

The good news is that every day belongs to the Lord. So, we can worship at any hour and on any day. Because every day, all day, is "The Lord's Day."

<u>NEXT</u>

In spite of the example of early Christians, people have argued over small things. Let's look at another example of big fights over small things.

PERSONAL Wisdom

CONFUSION

"There is something wrong with this church," he told the young people.

I asked him what was wrong with our church. He just wrinkled his face and said, "Get these chairs out of here." He said that every true church must have wooden pews. He said that his wife, who was White, refused to attend our church. Being Black, he came alone. He believed the church we attended together was not a true church. I wondered why he did not attend a White church.

He also demanded that everybody call him "Reverend." Young people in the church thought that a reverend was a person who knew what was right.

I had no intention of trying to change his mind. I knew that his heart was based on his admiration and fear of whiteness. But I was worried because he was going around the church talking to the young people. He said, "White churches are true churches. They have wooden pews."

I decided to try something. I asked him to go for a ride with me. I said, "Let's go to a White church." During the week, we walked into an empty White church sanctuary. And we saw chairs.

Reverend was shocked. He could not bring himself to condemn the White church the same way he always condemned the Black church. Both churches had the same chairs. I asked him what he thought. He gave me no answer. He still refused to say that Black churches were true churches. At least he stopped misleading the young.

His heart was still confused, but his mouth was shut.

NEXT

The experiences of children may be small things, but they have meaning. Check out the next tale.

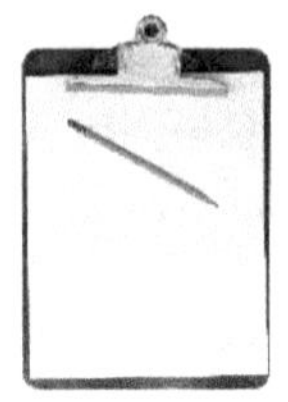

NEED A JOB?

I needed a job. I decided to try journalism. I had bombed out of the shoeshine business by messing up so many shoes. I found my niche in journalism. At rush hour, I stood at the subway stop and yelled, "Read all about it! The latest actions of the City Council. Get your newspaper here!" I think they liked my eight-year-old smile. Journalism was a successful career until I was cornered by a street gang. They took my day's "take."

So, I joined the street gang so I could grab other people's "take." You always have to adjust to different challenges.

By the time I was 14, I needed more money than I could get by taking the "take" of others.

I went to work for a bridal veil manufacturer. I was very good at delivering veils to stores, so I wanted a raise. But the owner of the bridal veil company would not renegotiate my contract.

I decided that delivering packages to corporate headquarters might be more profitable. I signed on to a messenger service. You had to make the delivery and get back to the dispatch office quickly or lose your job. I delivered small packages all over mid-Manhattan, even to the 95th floor of the Empire State Building. In a hurry to return to the dispatch office, I decided to run down the 94 sets of stairs. I decided not to wait for an elevator.

Soon, my legs got tired. But the doors were locked. I could not get back to the elevators. My desperate banging finally brought help. Banging does not make up for bad decisions.

In the 1950's, New York City was full of signs that said "N...s need not apply." I decided to look out of state. I thought, *Racial prejudice can't be everywhere.* My friend found an ad for residential movers across the Hudson River near the Lincoln Tunnel.

My buddy and I went to a New Jersey moving company. The man invited us in. He even gave us an application form to fill out. He said we have to be 18 to work for his company. He asked us how old we were. We lied.

After completing the interview, he took us into the warehouse. He showed us a refrigerator and said, "Let me see you carry this up this flight of steps." My buddy agreed to take one end. I would take the other. But the man said no. "You have to do it one at a time. Let me show you how." He wrapped a canvas belt around the refrigerator and pressed his back against it. He bent over, lifting the refrigerator onto his hips and walked up the flight. Then he came back down with the refrigerator. He said, "Let me see you do it."

We froze.

He said, "Don't call me, I'll call you."

We reported our accomplishment to our friends. We all agreed that New Jersey was a better place to work than New York. Although we never got the call, we were heroes. For the first time, a White man had shown us some respect even though he knew we were not 18.

What a guy!

34

<u>NEXT</u>

Sometimes Creator uses small experiences to build character in children. The next tale will explain.

THAT BLACK MAN

Ebbets Field was too small and too ugly for people to want to attend games. Besides, the Brooklyn Dodgers kept losing games. New Yorkers called them "the Bums."

Dodger executive Branch Rickey was desperate. He had to get more people into the stadium. There was no revenue from television. Radio didn't produce enough money.

The White population in New York City did not believe that Blacks were intelligent enough to play baseball. Branch Rickey thought that White people would attend to see a Black man fail. He also believed that the Black people would attend to watch a Black man succeed. If he got a Black man to play on the Dodgers, he would fill the stadium.

The Dodger organization knew of one Black Man who had spent two years at UCLA. He was drafted into the army and became a second lieutenant in a tank division. Maybe they could recruit him.

When the offer came, that Black Man and his wife Rachel decided to take the job. While he played baseball, Rachel did medical research at the Albert Einstein College of Medicine.

On the big day, both Blacks and Whites filled the stadium. The Dodger executive had been right.

To me, he was that Black Man out there among all those White people. Most of his own teammates did not like him. He seemed all alone. Taunting came from the stands. But that Black Man had more love than the haters had hate.

As he walked toward the tunnel after the game, White boys ran down to the fence to get his autograph. They had programs and pencils to write on. At seven years old, I didn't know what an autograph was. As that Black Man came up to me, I had nothing for him to sign. He paused. A full-face smile. A hand reaching through the fence. Grabbed my right hand. Shook it.

People think that I shook hands with him.

No.

Jackie Robinson shook my hand.

NEXT

Creatures of nature are not too small for Creator to consider. Creator has provided them with a home. We may visit, but it is their home.

WHOSE HOME IS THIS, ANYWAY?

That loud staccato rumbling was the sound of alligators. The Santee Cooper River Junction, half lake and half swamp. Home of water moccasins and alligators. But the fishing was good. We reeled in catfish as fast as we got hooks into the water. Cousin Coot, 14 like me, was good at it. He was a farm boy. Cousin Mamie Lee, 18, managed to catch a few. Aunt Jesse was doing well. But Uncle Sydney had known where to find catfish and was filling up a basket. I caught one; more than 12 inches long.

"Hook your two fingers under the bony prongs sticking out from the side of its head. Put your thumb in its mouth. Use your free hand to remove the hook."

Motionless catfish. Playing dead. As soon as I removed the hook, the monster twisted, somersaulted, and landed on the floor of the rowboat. The beast drove a bony spike deep into my bare big toe. Pain kicked high and hard, splashing the fish back into the water. That was the first adventure. The following Saturday was another adventure.

After we finished fishing, we slid our boat onto the beach. We were greeted by a six-foot moccasin slithering back into the water. It was on my side of the rowboat. The sleek black creature stopped, raised up to face me. Out of the corner of my eye, I saw Aunt Jesse slowly lifting a paddle. But before she could deliver a fatal blow to the fork-tongued menace, Uncle Sydney twice said,

"Put that paddle down!" I could not help staring into the eyes of the snake. None too soon, it eased itself down and swam off into the deep.

A third adventure was when we stayed on the lake section until after sundown. The boathouse was about 200 yards away. All we could see was its lightbulb hanging down by a wire.

Uncle Sydney operated the motor attached to the back of our rowboat. He put Cousin Coot on one side of the boat, me on the other. "Watch for stumps." I did not know that in order to create the lake, they had cut down trees. And some stumps almost reached to the surface. No stumps could be seen in the water, as black as ink.

Mamie Lee whispered, "Oh no," as the boat rode onto a stump and stopped.

"Coot, Bliese, do y'all know how to swim?"

We gave a feeble, "Yes, Uncle Sydney."

There were only two life jackets; one went to Aunt Jesse, the other to Mamie Lee. As the alligators exercised their bass voices, I wondered whether I could swim to the boathouse before getting caught. And what about the smooth swimming critter I met last week?

Uncle Sydney told everyone to get to the back. The nose of the boat went up. Uncle Sydney was big and strong, a man who never lost his nerve. He climbed to the front. Grabbed each side and rocked the whole boat from side to side. We slid off the stump. We were on our way. Until we met a second stump. The process was repeated.

Back in Harlem, I was asked whether I had gone fishing in South Carolina. "Yeah," as I pulled a piece of catfish spike from my blue toe.

NEXT

Sometimes letting go of a small thing is a big deal. You'll discover this in the following tale.

JACKET

Robbie and I were the two youngest members of the gang. Nevertheless, I was able to contribute my share for buying custom designed gang jackets thanks to my newspaper business. One of our members created the design. It was blue and gold with a profile of a cavalier topped with a beautiful feather. The blue and gold on one side could be reversed to show gold and blue on the other. It included the letters SAC: Social and Athletic Club.

We spent most of our time playing team sports and having dances in crowded living rooms. Yes, with the girls. Who were the girls? They were what churches call the ladies' auxiliary.

But they were not harmless. They carried the guns. Three boys walking down the street were sure to be stopped by a patrol car. Searched. But girls could carry the weapons to the staging site. No police stopped them. The girls were good at surveillance. And that made them good at tactical planning. The police seemed to be unaware of the role of the girls.

The jackets caused a lot of trouble. Since beauty is attractive, they caused everybody to pay attention to us.

One day, Robbie and I were playing handball against a wall. Two young guys rode up on bicycles. The leader opened his jacket to show us a pistol. He said, "You two guys are too young to be in the gang, but you let the Cavaliers know that when they come to Galvani tomorrow, come with their jackets and give them to us or don't come back to school."

We said, "Okay."

Eventually, everybody lost their jackets to the bigger gang except Robbie and yours truly. Robbie and I stopped wearing ours.

Later, I got it into my head to wear my jacket. I got on the IRT subway wearing my Cavalier jacket. At the other end of the car there were five young guys staring at me. I got up and went to my exit door, pretending to leave. Anybody standing at the exit door was standing in an enclosure. As the train pulled into the station, I was not visible to the five guys. They went to their end enclosure, ready to get off. I could not see them, and they could not see me.

The doors opened. I did not move. They, thinking that I was getting off, got off to wait for me and for my jacket. The doors closed and I was still standing in my exit enclosure. As the train pulled out of the station, I waved goodbye to the confused group as I glided past them.

When I started college, I did a very hard thing. I let go of my old jacket and my old friends.

<u>NEXT</u>

Seeing is not always believing. Check out the next tale.

"SEEING AIN'T ALWAYS BELIEVING"

ROGER: Ever see a homeless bum on the corner at a subway station? He's got two cardboard boxes set up to make a table. He shuffles two red cards and one black card.

ME: Yeah. It's called "Three-Card Molly." The bum plans to take money from everybody getting off work on payday at five o'clock.

ROGER: How does the bum do it?

ME: The homeless bum knows how many people think "Seeing is believing." But we must not only see; we must also observe.

ROGER: What does that mean?

ME: It means we must always seek to understand what we are looking at.

The bum yells, "Five will get you ten! Ten will get you twenty!"

ROGER: What I saw was the rush hour crowd passing. At first, nobody cared. They had cashed their paychecks. Ready for the weekend. Then a woman walked over to the table. She was dressed like a professional. She began to bet. Guess what? She won! Folk gathered around her.

ME: Others began to bet.

ROGER: Yeah. Everybody was winning. The professional woman kept pointing to the right card. But then, everybody began to lose. Professional Woman kept pointing to the wrong card. She became frustrated. The bum began to shuffle very slowly. But he still won.

ME: What did Professional Woman do?

ROGER: Homeless was looking around and yelling, "Five will get you ten! Ten will get you twenty!" Professional knocked one of the red cards to the ground. Professional quickly bent up one corner of the black card. Everyone saw what she did. They put down lots of money. Trying to win back what they lost.

ME: Did Homeless pick up the fallen card?

ROGER: Yes.

ME: Did Homeless see Professional knock down the red card?

ROGER: No. He just kept on yelling. He shuffled the cards. Everyone watched the black card with the bent corner.

ME: Did Professional point to the card with the bent corner?

ROGER: Yeah.

ME: And was it the right one?

ROGER: No, it wasn't.

ME: How do you explain what happened?

ROGER: I don't know. Because she did point to the bent corner.

ME: I'll explain. A skillful hand can do more than one thing at a time. When Homeless stooped down to pick up the red card, he bent one of the corners of that fallen red card. He unbent the black card when he began to shuffle. He left the red card bent. Then he shuffled. He collected a pile of money!

ROGER: Oh, wow!

ME: They tried to cheat him, but he cheated them.

ROGER: Yeah. And folk got mad.

ME: Now, do you think he could just walk away from them with all their money?

ROGER: No. Nobody said anything. They stared at him. Then a teenager in the back of the crowd yelled "Chickee!" The police were coming. Everybody ran away.

ME: Everybody except Homeless, right? Homeless calmly picked up his boxes. With Professional Woman on one side of Homeless and Teenager on the other, they walked away.

NEXT

We tried to keep our word. See how.

WE DID OUR PART

New York City woke me at three in the morning. Sirens were a hundred screaming monsters. The Nazi wolfpack submarines had arrived in New York Harbor. I had a job to do. Leap out of bed. Rush to the floor model radio. Turn the volume button all the way to 'off.' My brother ran around our apartment turning off lights and lamps. He was tall and he could reach everything. I was three. I couldn't reach switches. He was five and tall enough.

I stood with my back to the radio. The bare feet of my big brother barely made a sound. He joined me. Shoulder to shoulder, we stood in the darkness. We could not talk. We knew the Japanese soldiers were listening outside our window. We ran. We launched our bodies into the air, flying like Superman. Our bellies hit the waxed linoleum. We slid to safety under our parents' bed. Once again, our part done.

Daddy was already out of the house. He had his armband, his helmet, his gas mask, and his club. He would protect the family. Nazis could not beat our father, so we went to sleep under Mama's warm body.

Two years later, our Army came striding down Fifth Avenue. Daddy, my brother, and I were there to do our part. We yelled with all our might as the Marine drill team threw the rifle high.

They glided under it. The soldier in the last row caught it without looking.

We stomped our feet as the Women's Army Corps stepped onward. Bell-bottom pants of the sailors. Bars and stripes of the Army. Anchor symbols of the Coast Guard. No wonder men backslapped and women gave hugs and kisses. The suffering and sacrifice of war had ended. The boom of the bass drums, the blasts of the trombones, the shouts of the trumpets. Time for cheering! We did our part.

Then we heard the disappointment of the women talking to each other in the kitchen. They had built planes, tanks, and battleships. Now they were being told they were only good enough to fix breakfast. We listened to the bitterness of the soldiers in the living room. They had been appreciated as liberators abroad. Now they were despised as N...s at home. The men and women of that generation did not have a chance to do anything about their frustration. They were too busy making a future for us.

But we children remembered the complaints of our women. We children recalled the bitterness of our men.

When we got grown, we had to do our part.

That is why the women burned their bras.

That is why we marched from Selma to Montgomery.

NEXT

There are three kinds of leadership. Count them in the next session.

SELMA

The sun was melting the darkness. "Alright, it's time to go!" a man yelled. His voice made us willing to walk into the jaws of the dragon: Jefferson Davis Highway.

It was Tuesday. The Monday 300 had already covered their miles. We 300 had 23 miles to walk. Lewis F. Powell, of Virginia, was my walking partner. He was president of the American Bar Association. And years later, he became a Supreme Court justice.

The march was part of a larger plan to secure voting rights for every American.

The Communist Party of North America wanted to take over the Civil Rights Movement. They tried to take over our meetings. We stopped them.

The civil rights struggle of the 1960s involved both the younger generation, who had the new ideas and the energy, and the older generation with the experience and judgment. Our elders deserve more credit. They raised the money needed; they got attorneys to get us out of jail for free; they provided news helicopters over the marchers' heads to film the march and protect us; they pressed the politicians to do the right thing.

President Lyndon Johnson ordered the National Guard to protect us. But they were the Alabama National Guard. They hated us. All of us. The guards spat on the man in front of me. He was a White man wearing the collar of a minister. They did not call out loud. They just mumbled insults under their breath as we walked by. Their rifles were loaded. If we had reacted, we would be dead.

Fortunately, the leaders of the movement understood the three sides of leadership. They knew that there must be what the Bible calls a "vision." A vision is an idea that people consider very important. Somebody has to explain the idea. "Break it down." That person was Martin Luther King Jr. He called the vision his "dream."

But no dream can come true without a plan. The person who created a detailed plan was Wyatt Tee Walker. The plan showed the steps that led to success.

Dr. King had a certain personality, a certain way of thinking, a certain set of skills. Dr. Walker was different from Dr. King. Dr. Walker had a different personality, a different way of thinking, and a different set of skills. They were two very different people who deserve equal credit.

And then there was the third person. He had a different personality, a different way of thinking, and a different set of skills. That person possessed uncommon courage. He was Reverend John Lewis. JoaLewis locked arms with Martin and with Wyatt and simply said, "Let's go!"

<u>NEXT</u>

Are you a child, a teenager, or an adult? Examine yourself using the next tale.

GENERAL
Wisdom

Son

Would you like a piece of my sandwich? Sorry, I don't have anything to drink. Freight trains don't have food cars. Help yourself while I tell my story. I am headed home and I'll tell you why.

My father is wealthy. I decided to demand my share of my inheritance. My father said, "You are my child. I will give you your inheritance. Take care of yourself." I left home and traveled across the country.

Wait, listen, this freight train is slowing down. Men are jumping on. That one there looks afraid. He must be running away from a Christian lynch mob. Freight trains rescued many Black men from Christian terrorists. I escaped on a freight train a couple of times. Once in South Carolina and once in Alabama. I know how he feels.

Where was I? Oh, yes.

I spent money like water. I had a lot of friends. I went through a small fortune. When the money ran out, I had no more friends. I sometimes slept on a park bench. Sometimes under a bridge. Whenever I was hungry, I entered a men's shelter. I stood in many bread lines.

I moved from town to town. I learned a lot.

In Phoenix, I learned about the concept of a circle of seven generations. Some Indians told me that we are supposed to be responsible for the three generations that came before us. We must uphold their reputation. We must pave the way for the next three generations. And we are accountable for what we do with our own lives. We are a part of a circle of seven generations.

In Chicago, I read a book by Dr. Grady McWhiney. It was called *Cracker Culture*. I learned that some of us Black folk have been exposed to "Cracker culture." That culture despises education and work. That used to be me.

In Harlem, I talked with Malcolm X in his restaurant. He said that if a man does not respect women, he does not respect himself. I asked him to explain. He said such a man is a fool because his own mother was a woman.

In St. Louis, I spent a night in jail for vagrancy. A minister asked me, "What have you done for your mother lately?" I had no answer.

I realized what I had to do. I had to talk to my father.

I phoned my father. He asked me many questions. I told him everything that I had learned.

My father called to a servant, "Call the caterer so we can have a feast. Sonny is coming home."

My father then said, "A child takes care of no one. A boy takes care of himself. A man takes care of others. You, my child, are now a man. You're my son."

I understood what my father meant. That is why I'm on this noisy freight train. I'm headed home.

Where are you headed?

NEXT

Then, the big picture is helping others. Some musicians did that.
See for yourself, coming up next.

FREEDOM MUSIC

Charles strapped the saxophone to his body as he did his chores. He practiced in the fields. He practiced in the barn. He practiced as he walked with the cows back from the pasture.

When he played, he played the sounds of Mama's humming, Papa's shout, and Grandma's moan. And he never forgot the sounds of the birds of the forest.

But Mama was trapped.

No matter how hard Mama worked, no matter how big the crop she raised, at the end of each year, Mama sank deeper in debt. Charles was determined to earn money to free Mama from the evil system of sharecropping.

The only hope was to earn money in a big city. He wanted to play with the best. They were in Chicago. How would he get there?

He walked. He rode between the cars of freight trains. That way no one would steal his horn while he was asleep. He slept in bushes outside sundown towns. He went without eating. His love for Mama would not let him feel hunger. Thoughts of Mama prevented his feet from getting sore.

Times were tough. The White folk owned everything. They owned the money, the bars, the nightclubs, the recording studios, the radio stations, the musicians' union, the record companies, and the music shops. When all else failed to oppress us, they also had a Christian organization called the Ku Klux Klan.

Nevertheless, Charles had "a made-up mind" to succeed. One of the musicians he met found out that Charles called chickens "Yardbirds," so the musicians nicknamed him "Yardbird."

He practiced with the best. He performed with the best.

He paid for Mama to go free.

This tale is not really about one man. He represents the experiences of all the men and women of the jazz era. Those musicians liberated their family members from sharecropping. They played the song "Let my people go!"

Those musicians are songbirds we must honor.

Later in his career, the one they used to call "Yardbird" was called "Bird." He introduced a new style of playing the saxophone. His playing was greatly admired. Musicians decided to name the most famous jazz club in the world after him. It is called "Birdland." It's down on 52nd Street in Manhattan.

A tribute to Charlie "Bird" Parker.

Birdland is a reminder of the musical beauty of freedom.

<u>NEXT</u>

Some people have presented us with the wrong big picture. The following tale is an example of the wrong big picture.

NORWEGIAN JESUS

Look at this picture. Who is it?

I don't know.

It's a fellow named Cesare Borgia. He lived in 16th century Italy. And he was very angry.

About what?

His father, the Pope, had given his brother a high-level government position. It was a position that Cesare really wanted.

Wait a minute. You said his father was the Pope? I thought Popes did not get married. How could he have children. What's the word they use?

Celibacy. But the Pope had four children before he became Pope. He was a cardinal first.

But aren't cardinals priests? I thought priests didn't get married either.

That particular cardinal was very fond of the ladies.

I see.

Cesare was very fond of everything, especially himself. He became important, so he got a talented painter to paint a picture of him. He called the painting of himself "The Christ".

How did he become important?

He got his brother's position after his brother was murdered.

Did the people find out who did it?

No, it was an unsolved case.

After his picture was painted, did the people believe he was "Christ"?

No, because they believed that he had murdered his brother to get his brother's position.

Did anybody else paint "Christ"?

Dozens of other artists tried. They painted a lot of men and called each one "Christ." They hoped to become famous.

Did they become famous?

Only Michelangelo became famous for a statue of Christ.

Was that the end of all the paintings of Christ?

Not quite. Warner Sallman, a Norwegian-American came along in 1940. He got Catholic and Protestant publishers to print his painting of "Christ" on everything they published. On prayer books, bookmarks, hymn books, everything.

But was Jesus born in Norway?

No. He never set foot in Europe. But, thanks to the publishing companies, everywhere you look, you see Sallman's Norwegian "Christ".

That's true. My in-laws have the Norwegian "Christ" on the wall of their living room.

Recently, I came across a painting by Janet McKenzie called "The People's Christ". It is a masterpiece. It presents a universal Christ. Maybe everyone will now be satisfied.

<u>NEXT</u>

How did we get so confused about the wrong picture? Check out the big picture in the final tale.

WESTERN CIVILIZATION

My cousin just graduated from college. He says he's a Greek.

If he looks like you, he's a Black man.

He does look like me.

Then he is a Black man. Why do you think he calls himself a Greek?

I don't know.

It's because he was taught to admire the Greek people. By admiring the Greek people, he was taught to admire the White man.

But his fraternity brothers are Black men.

Their professors convinced them that everything important came from the White man.

Even the Christian religion?

Yes, so he falsely claims. And he spread these ideas all over the world.

How?

By putting those ideas in the colleges of his colonies. Remember, the European man controls a lot of colonies. He has had colonies in Asia, Africa, South America, North America.

How did he get so many colonies?

He used the gun.

Didn't they buy Manhattan Island from the Indians? The Europeans must have bought a lot from the Indians at a good price. They got Alabama, Mississippi, Michigan. The Indians must have been very generous.

No. They were dead.

Is that how the European man got land in Asia, Africa, South America, the Caribbean?

Yes. And don't forget Taiwan, Vietnam, Palestine, and Shanghai.

All by force?

Unfortunately. You see, if someone holds a gun on you, you give him your wallet. If someone holds a cannon on you, you give him your land.

Does his religion allow him to massacre people? You said Christianity is the White man's religion.

No, I didn't. I said the White man claims that it is his religion. Since it is not, he can interpret it anyway he wants.

How does he teach his interpretation of the Bible to everybody?

He uses something called the *Scofield Reference Bible*. He prints his interpretation of specific parts of the Bible, and he pushes that interpretation into the footnotes.

Can you put your footnotes into somebody else's book?

You are not supposed to. But they get away with it because nobody challenges them.

What do the footnotes say?

The footnotes say that you and I are an inferior race. We're not supposed to try to change anything while the White man waits for the Rapture. Before the Rapture happens, he can do whatever he pleases.

What is the Rapture?

It is an event in which Jesus comes into the world to rescue the White race. The White man will disappear and say, "I'm out of here." And we are left behind.

The Scofield footnotes say that? So, whenever someone purchases the Scofield Reference Bible, they are buying those teachings.

Right. It was a clever way to deceive a lot of people.

If the European man did not invent all knowledge, then where did Western Civilization come from?

Geometry came from ancient Africa. Appreciation for the mathematical concept of zero came from India. Understanding of the wisdom in nature came from North America. Insight into the human nervous system, the magnetic compass, and gun powder came from China. Knowledge of herbal medicine came from South America, Africa, and the Caribbean.

If all that knowledge came from all over the world, what explains the Europeans having possession of it and calling it Western Civilization?

Chief Justice of the United State Supreme Court, John Marshall, ruled that Western Civilization is legally valid because it came from the bloody edge of a sword.

He actually said that officially?

Yes. I say it this way:

It came out of the barrel of a gun.